AF333615

"Other Titles by R. Durand"

The Book of Months (1971), J. (1971),
The Old Man and the Monkey King (1972),
The Yes! Press Anthology (ed. 1972),
The Ages of J. (1973)

The Ages of J.

Robert Durand

Christopher's Books

Published by Christopher's Books
1819 Sycamore Canyon Road
Santa Barbara, Ca. 93108

Library of Congress Catalog Card No. 73-76636
ISBN 0-87922-020-1

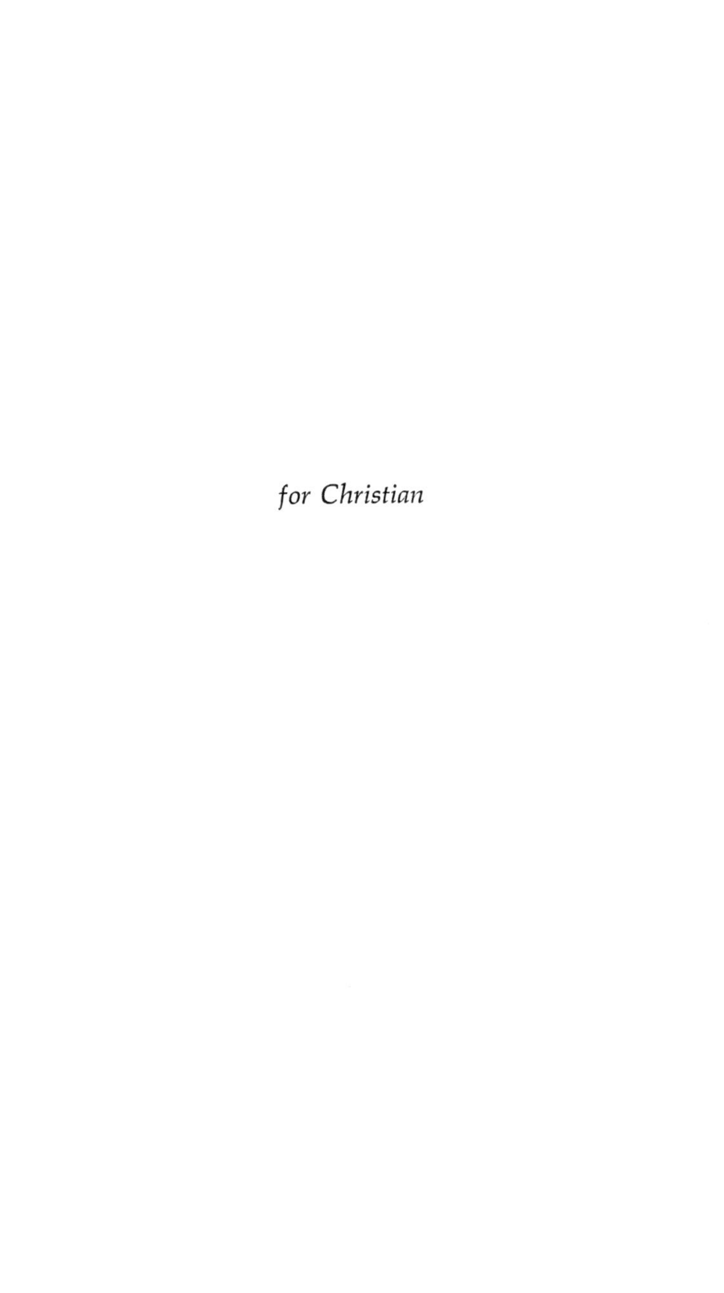

for Christian

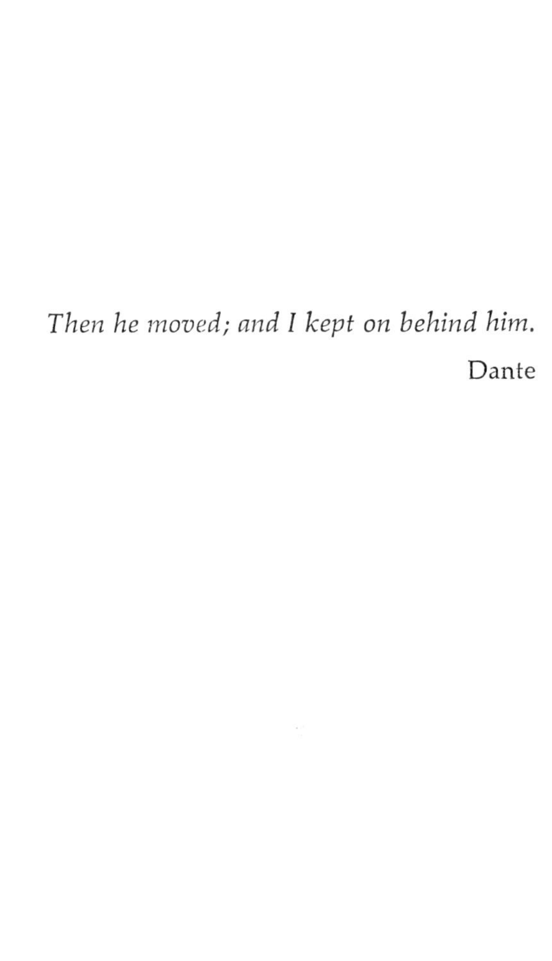

Then he moved; and I kept on behind him.

Dante

J. REVENANT

in the Stygian Chambers
we rented by
the month —
my J., scored like men are now,
on birdlike legs
and with smoky eyelids
comes, see him,
sinister lights glow through the hollows of
his cheeks.
He has the face of the predator owl,
disgruntled transvestite
of the night.
I've nothing to say to him,
we agree.
Raucous clouds.
Arms whapping like wings
against the awful walls.

We had to get out.

BIOPSY

And so
we decided to look into ourselves,
a part of his fluttering
heart, a piece
of my diaphonous iris.
We removed these sections from our
living bodies
and set them on the table
for examination.

We soon discovered
they possessed wills of their own,
began veering towards
each other,
and joined. My latent sight
was wondrous restored, J.'s
feelings.
This was the direction we were
moving in.

J. AND THE GHOSTLY CHOIR

It was Hallowe'en,
of course. One stroke
of the guillotine
past midnight
and we were miles away from civilization.
Into the Dark Wood
J. led me, down, down,
to a hidden amphitheatre.
"Sit here," he said and I sat
and the moon found me.
J. disappeared.
Nothing moved, nor I.
Clouds came then, fast, fast.
Still I waited.   The
wind rose.   And then...

I noticed J. in the
center of the glade, hooded,
holding aloft a bramble
torch to a host
of strange creatures
slipping in from deep shadows past him.
They formed a semicircle,
the light flickered
against them and they
were faceless.   At a wave
of J.'s torch, they broke
into a high canting.
I leaned to hear the eerie.

Another wave
and they stopped as
suddenly. J. played them
thus, on off on off on off.
And each time off, I
finally caught that one of their
number winked out, a silver
hole of moonlight
where he'd sung.
And then there were none.

"It's a little pleasure of
mine," J. said as
we wound our way out of the Dark Wood.
"A gathering of friends."
The sky was growing lighter
and it was
only later that he thought
to refer to this concert
as The Guillotine Rhapsody.

WE HAUL GARBAGE

Another lark it was!
We dressed in grime and dungarees
and heavy leather gloves.
And made our rounds.
We stopped at a house
and hauled off a marriage.
We stopped at a church and came away
with twenty loads of sins.
This delighted us!
We sweated with exuberance.
At a military installation, we
scooped up Nike;
at the World Bank, all
the middle-aged ingots.
We continued our rounds
and ran soon out of room
at the landfill.
We had gorged ourselves
and it was not yet lunchtime.
We ended by hauling each other away,
arm-in-arm,
leg-in-leg.
We were ripe, ripe,
ripe for the taking!

THE CHESS MASTER

He wanted to play real pieces.

J. and I volunteered
and I would be queen and
J. fancied he'd like to be the dark
digonal bishop. We
were arrayed along the
field with our own forces
against those of the opposing army.
We were moved.
We were not compromised.
He was leading us brilliantly,

that arrogant prodigy
master —
but just as he was sure of
decisive victory, J., J.
wheeled and struck down his own king!
In an instant,
the war had been treacherously
joyously lost!
That arrogant prodigy blind-sided
master — little he knew
to not beware
the blow of a rogue bishop!

CYPHER

Fk fktk gstguzyclsocpsyo pmk xjdduk vi c ykf
etkcz ivt c ysomp'n esnptcgpsvy . . .

C mvuvgcjnp   gvynjzke c gspb xkvxuke
fspm c zsuusvy tkxusgcn vi vjtnkulkn.
Sy vyk ysomp.   Pmk cst fcn gmctoke fspm
npcpsg gtcgwusyo kyktob cye   eknptjgpsvy.
Sy c ikf ausnesyo nkgvyen,
mjnetken vi pmvjncyen fktk wsuuke.   Ajsuesyon
fclktke, pjzauke.   Pvpcu vlktfmkuzsyo
nsukygk nkppuke vlkt cuu.   C pmvjncye
iczsusct aveskn, cuu   pmkp tkzcsyke,
cuu esiiktkyp cokn,   njpzauke
cavjp sy jppkt cszuknnyknn,
zjpk,   fspm kbkn lcnpub kzxpb.
Cye pmky vyk cp c pszk gvuucxnke,   ekce.
Q. njgguzake pv pmk mvttvt.
Iuke,
ajtysyo.   Fk mce yv nvujpsvy.

HOLOCAUST

We were circumnavigating the puzzle of a new
dream for a night's distraction . . .

A holocaust
consumed a city peopled
with a million replicas of ourselves.
In one night.
The air was charged with
static crackling energy and
destruction. In a few
blinding seconds, hundreds of thousands of us
were killed.   Buildings
wavered, tumbled.
Total overwhelming
silence settled over all.
A thousand familiar
bodies, all that remained,
all different ages,
stumbled about in utter aimlessness,
mute,
with eyes vastly empty.
And then one at a time collapsed,
dead. J.
succumbed to the horror.
Fled, burning.
We had no solution.

THE PICKTHANK

He attached himself to us.
Or we to him.
A miserable fellow,
a puling twisted wretch
of a fellow, along
a dusty backroad one year.
A thick tongue, a crooked spine
with a game leg that poked
out at a grimacing angle —
these he had.
We took him on to
carry our baggage and at
first were immensely
pleased with ourselves
and called him our
familiar.

But he soon turned
sycophant, slavering, fondlesome.
J. dismissed him
abruptly one evening.
The fellow
skulked off up the road
and out of our sight.
When we followed in
the morning, we found him dead,
his whole chest stove in.

Out of the shattered
cavity a seamy powder was being
lifted up and borne
across the desert
on the hot dawn wind.

"What do you figure it was?" I
felt obliged to ask.
"Greed," J. said, moving
away from the writhing talcum.
"Very distinctive taste.
Acquired."

CONCERNING THE ROC
AND THE INFANTA

From another dream we had,
a roc,
wearing the plumage of J.,
wings spanning the bowl of the sky
and already heavy with prey for its insatiable
offspring, tore
nonetheless a small infanta,
with a face unmistakably like mine,
from her tutelage.
Bore her screaming to the craggy heights.
The eyrie was tall, wind-buttressed.
Seven days and nights
the seizure
of feasting lasted
before the creature left to return to her
hunting.
The fledglings slept,
confident of their great mother's success.
One of the young
turned in its sleep, stretching its
new wings.
We saw how its feathers were adorned
with strips
of my hair and clothing.

J. turned his eyes away
and I knew
at this point
how dreams might or might not alter
the course of our future lives.

CODPIECE

There was an art and a fine fashion
to the making
and wearing of them
that challenged us both.
J. argued giddily for their return,
though we were not
in disagreement over the matter.
We set to work,
and it was a game at first,
a contest between us —
who could design and wear
the most belligerent codpiece in
existence.

We worked closeted away
from each other,
so as not to borrow or steal.
The lamps had burned
low when I
heard J. shout exultantly.
I knew he'd done,
and hurried to finish
and we met on the field of honor.
O   J.! — he had fashioned
a masterpiece,
a miniature in natural oils of the
shaking head of Medusa,
snakes bursting and seething like rich foliage
from the buttoned-up eye
of his loins.

But the *coup de grâce,*
the *pièce de résistance* of his creation,
were her eyes — they followed you
everywhere.
Mm, I was envious
and in awe,
and yet felt I still had a chance
in the game.
I unveiled my own,
padded, embroidered, laced in
cloth-of-gold
along the edges,

and J. gasped aloud —
for it was the Creation I'd sewn,
Buonarotti's,
line for line, tone for tone.
And though it irked him extremely
to do so,
J. extended his congratulations
to me.
It was only the second time I
had bested him.
But it brought about
the end of our game and was the last
time we ever
wore codpieces.

THE BERGSCHRUND

Gilles died.
He was the goat of the slopes
and had known J.
from first infancy.
His frozen unreachable remains
lay in a
deep Bergschrund
at the ten thousand foot level.
We climbed to it,
a lonely hopeless vigil that led
nowhere.
I could not assuage J.'s grief.
A day later he hiked
back down, with instructions
again that I was to wait for him there,
above the world.
Ice formed without mercy
over the goat-head of Gilles.

When he returned hours later,
J. drew from his pouch
the still warm and throbbing horns
of a mountain ram
and blew each one once,
loud clear notes that rang in the
thin airs.
Gilles dropped from sight.
At the ten thousand year level,
will the Bergschrund
have retreated enough?

CURARE

For years we ate it
as an erotic derivative,
building up a strange connection
that let us flow
& grow ever stronger into each other.
Neural flooding
became a constant pleasure
we could not forbid. . . .
Even now
there are the
peculiar after-effects,
those uncontrollable muscular
transports.

We are rumored
to be the only carriers of such
a tonic. We leave it at
that, though the
old doctor of Strychnos
might have noted . . .

J. READS THE DUINO ELEGIES

For beauty is nothing
but the beginning of terror we are just barely able to endure

Everything he brought the nun
designed to please her.
She would none.
J. fumed. Strolled the rim of the
lake alone, shrouded in a fog
of moods. He returned that night.
There was to be an eclipse
early, early the next morning, he said.
And he strapped her to the mast of the
little sailboat, her head shaved,
her eyelids taped open.

At dawn the sun climbed into the sky.
He cast the boat adrift; she
fainted. All the while I said
nothing. At last when the terrible
darkness came and the stillness
of the birds, and the boat
listed about in a small slow circle
in the lake's center . . . when I
saw that this
was to be the extent
of the experiment, I asked J.,
"What are you doing?"

"Testing the poet," he said,
"transforming the thought into
dumbshow."
"And?"

He shrugged.
"I am able to contain
her terror. But then she is not
as beautiful as I had hoped."
He was walking off.
It was left to me to
wreak a conclusion.

SOPHIE, THE SEA, THE NOON

We had entered our middle years
— come once more to
the end of the land
and the knocking battering sea —
J. clinging to the fire — I
found a cave
at the lip of high tide
— dark, warm, a pocket
against the wind,
a gathering place for driftwood —
somewhere in the back

I stumbled and picked up
the whorl of wood that caught me
— it was Sophie!,
caricatured, cartooned,
cracking — I knew at once she looked
this way in life by now! —
ran, I, crying nonsense,
gibberish to the past,
down to the fire
and threw the cruel wood in —
it broke out
in instant sparks
and gave off a scent I'd nearly forgotten,
of the musty cabaret
where she'd sung and danced,
where — J. looked up
suspiciously —
tide was in.

THE GARROTING

After all,
the opportunity did not arise every
day.

An order
of extremist monks, cloistered
in cone-shaped dwellings on the fringes
of society, and claiming
descent from a singular traveler
and a bright star
in Cassiopeia's girdle,
hired us to execute
their rare rite of succession.
We could not demur.

The method was this:
ascendancy by strangulation,
iron collars were fitted to the pair
of eligible necks.
We turned the screws,
the heads bloated,
nearly burst. The rightful heir
became discernible only
when Cassiopeia herself bent to stay
his dying
and the collar flew asunder,
spewing alien alphabets
of sounds across the ground.

J. pursed his lips in thought,
frowned.
I followed suit.
We listened again.
The story had credence,
and it *would* explain our long absence
in that section of the
memoirs.

SATORI WINDOW

for Kermit Shafer

J. brought home a peculiar window
one time
when we'd nothing left
to watch
and placed it on a blank space
of wall like a painting.
A paper window, but such that,
as the hours progressed,
we saw the changing sky pass through it.
Long vertical strips
of clouds and nights
and days. A horizontal bar of white
that might have been the sea.
Vast distances
and time. The diamond
beginnings of two similar boys.
Those we knew and did not know
appeared and vanished
in an erratic
and disturbing display
between the cracks in the strips
of the hanging sky.
Beyond it, life hesitated.

When it showed finally
the reluctance of time to hold us
together, or
at all,
we rolled it up and tucked it away.
We are leery
of windows.

THE CONJURE ROOM

Our great Salamander Murders
were occurring at the time the exhibition
came to town. We went
anyway. Entered together and
sat in two chairs placed
back to back. The room
pulsed with a low violet iridescence.
We were alone.
The door hummed shut. I glanced
down momentarily ... and
started, shaken. From out
of my genitals a large yellow-and-green
spotted salamander's head
flowered with frightening
realism. I hesitated
to touch it and called
out to J. But no answer
came. And I
couldnt turn around.
The room turned instead, lazily,
floor into ceiling into wall.
Two beautiful glistening feet
braced themselves against
my thighs. My
breath came short. "J.," I called
again. "J.!" A long shining
black ridge marked the
creature's spine, the beginning
of the moist and blunt-tipped
tail. Its head craned

around to fix me.   Small
perfect eye pools.   I was aware
of quiet water.
Back legs rose from
my testes while forelegs
climbed upon my chest.
The room continued to waft
and the salamander's head
swayed back and forth before my face.
I thought of victims.
Its breath gave off
a pleasant reek of damp summer
vegetation.   Mouth
opened wide.   I began
to fear.   Its tongue flicked, leaving
a dab of sticky saliva on
my chin . . . my chin.   For
some reason I groaned aloud.
My hands were useless.
It spoke, "You have the right
to remain silent . . . "
The voice was J.'s.
I looked for the door

AT THE SALON OF
MME. DE POMPARTIER

We turned up
in a photograph taken at the salon
of Mme. de Pompartier.
Neither of us, pouring over that stack
of keepsakes, though, recalled the
capricious picture
itself being taken.

J. reclined crosslegged atop an inlaid wood
dresser, wearing a tall black hat
and a black cravat, reading.
My nose was buried
in Mme.'s sumptuous violet-scented bosom.
Mme. was naked to the waist.
In a gilt-edged mirror,
we could see the photographer hunched
to his task.
Behind him (the crux of the matter!)
a hooded figure
began to administer a deathblow to
the man's skull.
Ah I remember —
J. and Mme. and I were the diversion!
Yes, in fact,
we had even commissioned the
murder,
a specialty of the House of Mme.

He was a frivolous man, that picture-
monger, a boor,
speaking as he did in rhymed couplets —

and so we showed him how knife
could rhyme out the ruinous end of his cretinous life.

A BOY OF NOTORIOUS CHARMS

A usurper,
a boy of notorious charms, attempted
to step in
between J. and I! To take
my place, or his!
I think J. was more astonished
than I.
We moved decisively, with cooing gestures,
warm lodgings, spinning the net.
The young fool fell.
Piece by piece, we stripped him
of his charms, his looks,
his youth,
and sent him back, a mass
of blisters and bleeding, unable
to hold himself erect
thereafter,
and pinned to him a note for his masters.
"Let that be a lesson!"

PAS DE DEUX OF THE FAUNS

"to the lascivious pleasings of a lute"

Horn dance!
Goat dance! We let
ourselves out for hire and toured
with a group of boy musicians
piping
and playing for us.
I'd wear the horns (same horns that J.
had blown to the death of Gilles)
and spirey ears,
and J. 'd strap to himself
the cloven hooves and spotted tail.
Dance spread
with fame. Dowagers clamored
for us, apartments were too small.
Moved to parks
and boulevards and
hilltops.
Dance spread, same dance . . .

Failing health and the age
of the music eventually brought us
to a halt.
Those,
and the wordly destruction of the myth
of Pan.
It was a time, actually,
when we began to dismember our own
myth. . . .

THE CLOCK MERCHANTS

The further we got along,
the more we began to horde clocks,
vast timepieces tocking
away the measured dying of our hours.
We had assembled the definitive
collection.
They hung and rested everywhere
in our rooms,
on the walls and windows,
from the ceilings and in sunlit
and shadow-struck niches.
The sound could be deafening, cacophonous,
as only an invasion
of time might be.
Water-clocks and wind-watches,
sundials and
chronometers geared to the moon and cold —
all elements were represented.
We dealt only in time as
our time grew less.

One day we sold the entire lot
at auction.
It fetched us
another couple of years.

A FLOW OF SPELLBINDERY

In matters of bright adornment, I suppose,
our way was sporadic.
I favored rings,
J. secret hidden trinkets of lewd
and exotic design.
But we were always losing them
or forgetting them or
changing them.
It took the sight of
an old Haitian sailor to remind us
of the possibilty in
tattoo.

We hurried to the harbor district
and found a leaning
darkened shop to our liking.
The fee was arranged.
The one-eyed proprietor
turned out to be an artist of the needle,
and what we had asked him for
no easy feat.

These scenes upon our backs
were worked to
appear and disappear
according to our proximity to each other.
We let them grow dim,

too dim.

THE ANEMONE

for Dennis Alexander

Anemone.
The anemone.
We fingered it in our senility.
We ravaged it.
Day after day we went back
to it, sometimes together, and some-
times alone.
It had the most perfect orange
and green vulva
either of us had explored.
Inadvertently, we let jealousy in.
Bickering, deceitful, obscene —

no wonder, then,
how we came to destroy it
in one fit, an actual
paroxysm
of desire. J. felt afterwards
wet tendrils about his throat
while I, I
felt suffocation.

Anemone.
The anemone.
We were too old for it.

ALCHEMIES

for J.

Metals, J., metals, the both
of us.
Do you have that sense, too, and of
our eternal tireless efforts
at transmutation?
Ah, the
performances we've enacted on our
persons!
Life prolongation!
What delectable irony!
I note with some curiosity and pleasure
how we have always been
outside history.
Men will not note
our demise, nor their instruments
be able to record it.
We have walked
as Mayan astronomers and men
of the Dog Soldier Society
alike; lived above
and below, and seem to be aging
at last
because of careful miscalculations.
Metals,
metals, J.
What's your guess?

INTAGLIO

In a lucid moment there towards
the end,
we had a thought for the future
and decided that,
instead of casting wills,
we would cast our own deathmasks.
From the cooling molds
we took positive impressions.
A startling thing was revealed:

Out of my negative form,
came the positive
of J.
And of his, that of me.
We were then unable, naturally enough,
to fit the originals
to our own faces,
only to the other's.
J. called this
the psychology of the *a priori* personality.

ECDYSIS

"Let's buy that!" that building,
that dark museum.
We did,
and J. renamed it
The Vomitorium. It was full
of the wreckage of our
species.
We quickly gave all the items
their walking papers.
Presently we were
the only ones left in the high empty halls,
and the next step
was the most obvious of all.
Without glance
or reflection, we parted, J. by the one
exit, I by the other.
It was winter, and quite old.
We had shed the last there
was to shed
and have not seen each other
                since.

THE EYE OF THE NEEDLE

So we moved in excess
of sunlight and darkness,
one and the other, interchangeably.
Traveling as we most often did
the long route
of the *Shao Yin,*
meridian of the hand, to
the heart.
Sickness, love . . . were in
the heart of each of us.
— And the remaining meridians,
into the forbidden points
and the Lo points
and those of
connection, source,
sedation, tonification,
in efforts to either heal or
anesthetize ourselves,
this J. and I.
We are full yet of the violent
tastes we met along
the ways.
We rode the floating pulse,
again
and again.

I am the *Hao* needle,
and J. the *Huo*.
If you would understand these matters,
know that the
paths were divisible.

POSTCARD TO CALAIS

O and I remember his mad snide laughter at the story of the burghers of Calais who had saved the lives of their port by sacrificing their own to a conquering general. He felt it his duty to send the whole town a recriminatory postcard; read:

"Citizens of Calais: You have betrayed yourselves, you have betrayed me. Better you should all have died than be remembered for the Six Fools — nay, the Six Clowns who bargained your continued existence. Death by proxy, indeed! And Rodin, your chronicler, Rodin was a fat old sentimentalist. I call his style mock-heroic. This communication is ended. (signed) J."

There was, almost of course, no reply. Calais continues unchanged, like J.'s scornful laughter, and this should tell you something further about him.

CHRYSALIS

From the solitude
I have come to understand in these closing
months,
the feeling grows that the roll
of the early years,
the full anarchic pageant, was only imaginal,
a larval and quiescent state
that
unpredictably led us nowhere,
my companion and I.
Split now
beyond each other's reach and
possibility.
All the youthful flirtations and curses —
for what?
this rattling in the throat?
this gloomy pitiful preoccupation with
empty doorways?
No,
I think not. And yet, then,
what else if not?
The illusory watery
memory
of that elegant wheel
he always insisted we rode,
spinning through the dark, spokes of light
against the absolute
Bleak?

No, not that either.
Stand back!
I had not considered dwindling!
J.! — J.!

Dear —, (J. wrote me once from the country of his old age)

I am living quietly here, subtly, and enjoying to my sur-
prise amongst the villatic local populace the sweetest of
all reputations — that of avatar. Oh, I know this will
amuse you. They are so accessible, these people; and yet
they do not plague me. I write you from a delirious state,
for three nights ago...let me tell you! Three nights
ago, my friend, I discovered a new strain in myself, a
canal dark with unexplored juices! I was agitated, agi-
tated to the point of distraction. She is, I think, but
fifteen years old! She dreamed of me, my face filled her
dream. I felt it suddenly in my study while revising some
childhood journals; seeking me out. The old fires awak-
ened that had lain so long dormant. I found in me, oh my
friend, my very good friend, found in me the condition
of incubus! Tears of joy welled up in my eyes. I flew to
her. The thread of her dreams was strong. I felt myself
shrinking in size — yes! till I stood only two feet tall.
I entered through her window, I was without substance.
She slept beneath an indigo eiderdown, the smells of
sleep upon her trembled me! My fingers shook, I looked
at them, they were transparent, and my arms, I could see
through my whole trunk. I pulled back the covering
from her slight form, dizzy. I recalled our journey to the
underworld, the white stains, the thin air, the closeness,
how we had never been so penetrated. Her nightgown
was cottony, mussed. The odor of her sleep crazed me!
I reached down for her. She was increasingly beautiful!
And I bit off a long lock of her hair and tied it through
my earlobes. Their dangling incensed me further. She
stirred. I took my time, I dwelt through her room awhile.

Looking for her keepsakes, her little treasures, sitting in her chair, standing in her closet surrounded by her clothes. Yes yes, to answer your wondering, her dream continued! I returned to her and gently, so gently disengaged her from her nightdress. Oh, she was of cameo proportions, my friend!...how shall I betray her innocence and unguessed charms to you? For I would. I would bring you her! We do not need to forgive each other! Ah! there was a slight flutter, in, of, her stomach! I lay down upon her. The night rang! Her dreams pounded, she stirred to life, a breeze rustled the curtains, her mouth opened slightly! To me! My friend, my friend! I pierced her, the night was ringing! Pain streamed between us, I stifled her cry, sucking it down into my throat, the pleasure was unbearable! Such a ringing! I crept from her! Her dream was on fire! I saw our juices convolute, running through her body; they were in mine. I was elated, fascinated; I followed the course of her chemicals through me. I took form again; weight regained. I crept from her. I have not returned to her. They say, in the town, that she has grown lethargic and sick, that at night now a strange fever laces her brow. Her sleep is troubled. During the day, I drop by to pay my respects, but she says nothing, recognizes no one. She has a younger brother! Oh, my friend, I know you will understand!

With fond regards,

J.

OF FLAMES

Given the nature of flames,
we have been as varied,
   you, strange man,
and I. Cold,
black, fired with radiant intemperance
as two moxa cones
or a pair of gelatinous suns
might be.

    Let us,

by way of ending, then,
and if you've
no objection, be placed
upon each other and there left to burn
and afford such great
or feeble light
as we shall be ever
called upon again
to need.

THE AGES OF J.

The rings of age around his heart —
we both saw them
spreading, dark at the core,
lighter where they
touched me.
In the dream he is a soft
and sinewy tree
of white wood,
and I am some vine trailing
over him.
We lose sight of earth and sky,
they are the same.
The rings deepen in J.,
I can not keep up with them.
This is the last I have to report.

Other titles in Christopher's *Hip-Pocket Series* include:

1 / *The Ages of J.* by Robert Durand
2 / *First Hunger* by Jo Anne Lee
3 / *Coyote Tantras* by Barry Gifford
4 / *Cool Zebras of Light* by Robert Peters

One thousand copies printed by Gary Albers,
August 1973, Santa Barbara.
Design by Melissa Albers.
Number One in Christopher's *Hip-Pocket Series*.